Detroit. Silent is [...] experience all its own. It we[...] any American city ever has, and even declared bankruptcy. But this metropolis is rising once again, a beautiful playground complex to approach, no matter who you are. Some stayed during the storm; most arrived after.

A gallerist duo is helping artists keep their ownership, a producer feels lucky just to be accepted, an Afro-futurist is giving back to the city's legacy, a fashion geek is reaching out to designers, and an investor and his architect are imagining a new Detroit. They show us a city evolving and fighting to stay true to itself.

Feel the complexity, uncover its many truths, and get lost in Detroit.

Belle Isle rests on the Detroit River, nestled between Michigan and Ontario. A beautiful natural preserve with the oldest aquarium and oldest continually running conservatory in the United States. There are beaches and nature trails galore, and it's gorgeous all year round. Find metre-thick frozen waves crashing against the shore in winter, or serene amber thickets in the fall. There's always room for the outlaw here too, as you drive around this island loop you are bound to notice the peaking pointed huts tucked away behind the shrubs. This is Belle Isle's secret treasure: a long decommissioned zoo that the canals run through. It's the urban kayaker's wet dream.
• Aquarium and Conservatory, 3 Inselruhe Ave, Belle Isle, belleisleconservancy.org

Oakland Avenue is not the most vibrant street in Detroit, but inside one grey brick building a historic bath house seems to have come straight out of a David Lynch movie. Red carpets and antique bells welcome you and for $30 you can stay from late in the afternoon till 10pm and enjoy this banya from the early 1930s. Rooted deep in the culture of the Eastern European Jewish community, the Detroiters know to ask for a platza. If you do, be ready to get beaten with oak leaves.
• Schvitz Health Club, 8295 Oakland Ave, New Center, schvitzdetroit.com

From Underground to Above Board

Past and Present

Food | Farm to Cake

This quaint homestead has been perched on the edge of Indian Village for over 50 years. What was originally Elmo's Fine Foods, is now under new ownership by Molly Mitchell who has filled the kitchen with roses and organic locally-grown produce, meat, dairy and grain. *Rose's Fine Food* works with Detroit's Urban Farms to help keep this new economy of over 1,500 urban farms alive. The "Staff Favorite" features all of the harvests carried through the seasons so that you can literally get a taste of Detroit.
• Rose's Fine Food, 10551 E Jefferson Ave, Indian Village, rosesfinefood.com

Second Opus

In this ancient radiator shop chef Brad Greenhill from Takoi is starting his new adventure. Here he offers predominantly plant-based dishes inspired by Mediterranean cuisine. He only uses a wood-fired grill and a wood-burning oven. A limit that challenges his creativity. You'll choose from a variety of small dishes for $9 each—that kicks off with flatbread served alongside chickpeas, farm cheese, or lamb. For the ones who are really willing to experience *Magnet* fully, the $65 per person menu is the way to go and is always a surprise since the chef changes it up based on the season's peak ingredients. Whichever you're coming for, you'll dive into this blue tile and walnut hall—a version of a modern diner where the most simple dish reaches new ground.

• Magnet, 4848 Grand River Ave, Core City, magnetdetroit.com

Cocoa Island

Every little kid dreams of living in a world made of chocolate. While most of us grow out of this fantasy, Alexandra Clark never did. After getting an MBA in Agricultural Economics with a focus on cocoa farms, Clark came back to her hometown and opened her very own chocolate shop, where she acts as lead chocolatier. Now, one might not expect the midwest to be the home of the hottest chocolate diva, but rest assured it is. Handmade, hand filled, hand packaged right in front of your eyes. Whether the flavour is Strawberry Balsamic, High Tea, Killer Cereal, or Crème Brulée you can't go wrong at *Bon Bon Bon.*

• Bon Bon Bon, 11360 Joseph Campau Ave, Hamtramck, bonbonbon.com

Food **On the Beaten Path**

The best is sometimes in the most challenging neighbourhood. Almost at the border of Detroit and Highland Park, a neon sign will come into view. Although Detroit is changing very fast, this institution isn't going anywhere soon. The Timmer family built the place brick by brick and still runs the show af' r 62 years. That's the story of this lan mark: a family-owned business ma...ing food for "regular folks," offering homemade donuts from a bygone era of epic quality.

• Dutch Girl Donuts, 19000 Woodward Ave, Palmer Woodscom

Night | **Easy Bake**

About 86 years ago, you would have come here just to eat a simple sandwich, and a few years later, to see some of the best jazz musicians alive. Nowadays, it's soul food and the new generation of musicians. The bar is still the same as it was, hugging the stage. You can't miss it, driving up Livernois: an Art Deco black and white sign with a traditional marquee announcing who's playing each night.

Inside, the piano-shaped bar is painted with a keyboard motif that gives you a sense of what's to come. This is where you just sit back and let yourself get carried away by the sound.
• Baker's Keyboard Lounge, 20510 Livernois, Green Acres, theofficialbakerskeyboardlounge.com

Shop | **Make a Wish**

You often hear about the decline of the textile industry in 1970s America, but you rarely hear about the once booming wax industry. Gratiot Avenue, which used to be lined with butchers and candle shops, now only has one of each. Welcome to *Discount Candles* where they know that getting used to praying can be difficult and requires a proclivity for religion. But fret not! The power of candles has got your back. Light one for good luck, better sex, or a hex. They're assured to fulfill your needs, whatever they are.
• Discount Candles, 1480-1482 Gratiot Ave, Eastern Market

11

Zachary Saginaw AKA Shigeto
is a modern techno artist signed
by Ghostly International and
born in Ann Arbor Michigan,
but he'll tell you that he was
raised on a healthy diet of corn
flakes and Detroit. Now, alongside his brother, he owns
Portage Garage Sounds, an
indie-label based in Hamtramck
which is changing the fabric
of the neighbourhood by working with local kids

Shigeto, Music Producer

True Sounds

As an artist of all genres Shigeto explores and curates Detroit's late-night crowds and knows what is still representative of the city's true music legacy. The artist revealed some clues to help traverse this hidden urban terrain

So, you are from Ann Arbor: a city not far from Detroit. What brought you here?

Yes, initially I grew up in Ann Arbor. It was always a dense and vibrant musical community of all genres across the board. It's where I learned about jazz and how to play drums. I went to NY, and then London, where I started to produce, then back to NY. Over there I was trying to get on Ghostly, the first indie label from Ann Arbor. I was a kid when they started, I was a fan, and I watched them grow. It was a dream of mine to work with them. They sponsored innovative music that wasn't mainstream. It was the time of raves with those weird flyers and specialised logos made just for one party. After a moment I was able to convince them because I got to a point where I was sustainable. But I was still in NY and living in a box, paying so much money for something I didn't even own. I wanted to be home, I wanted to save, I wanted to build, I wanted something bigger than myself and to have a sense of community.

What attracted you to this city?

Detroit is my biggest musical influence from jazz to motown, hip hop to techno, house to soul, funk to punk and rock. It's all fucking here! I was here to see the roots like Parliament and Slum Village. Here, they don't care, they just make. These cats put out records in the fucking hoods without any money. It all depended on how much you cared, and how this music could be physical. Even now there's more independent labels putting out records then places selling groceries. I came back to be local with the people who stayed here and to learn more about what I hold so dear. The most important thing for me is to work with the community. I'm producing 12 inches of dance music

here in Detroit. But what I really want to express is that: I am not Detroit. I was given the blessing to be here, but I am not a Columbus of new Detroit. I hate how under-valued this city is.

What would you say to a tourist coming to the city?

If you come to Detroit you'll be nervous. The dance music is incredible everywhere you go. But the whole world is talking about it, everyone wants to know. So if you want to know... just come see for yourself! Respect the culture, and appreciate how delicate it is. Walking around taking "ruin porn" photos with your camera is going to make people look at you, and not in a good way. Hang out with locals as much as you can. Not me—real locals. Not long ago, we booked Hugo Capablanca from Berlin. After the set, he came to us and said with tears in his eyes "I don't feel this way in any other city in the world." The DJs really get it because they feel the crowd. They feel the people.

Detroit is changing very fast. How do you feel about that?

I can't speak for Detroit. No doubt, Detroit is changing fast. Look at Berlin, it's almost turned into a place that is fake. Detroit will not always stay the same. I opened my studio in Hamtramck with my brother. Now this space has to integrate honorably without alienating the community. That is why we are doing ceramics here with the kids too. I let people use the studio to record for free. That's the only way you can respect the changes, the divide of money and the races.

Who are the DJs you would recommend here?

Mike Banks from Underground Resistance, Kenny Dixon Jr, Waajeed. They are not the oldest

The authentic Duly's Place Coney Island in Mexicantown

but they are interacting with their community. Mike would wear his coveralls and help somebody with their garage. People are doing that in an environment that has been exploited for so long. It's very sensitive.

You live in Hamtramck, a little pocket very different from the rest of the city, how would you describe it?

Hamtramck reminds me of Queens in NY, it's primarily Yemenis and Polish people. It's family-oriented, little streets, little businesses, only a few big corporations which are still local. Kids are running around everywhere, looking into the studio window. It's an escape from the main environnement but just next to it. Little bars, little restaurants and a huge art community.

What are the places you would recommend in this neighborhood?

The best place here for food is *Yemen Cafe*. Order the lamb fahsah and the special bread. There's also *Motor City Sports Bar*, which has great bar food. I love the cevapi, a sausage with feta cheese and pita. *Menjo's* is great for good little shows.

What are the most authentic places?

Obviously Detroit is well known for its Coney Islands, the traditional fast food chains with chili hot dogs. The best late night Coney Island is *Duly's Place* in South West. If you are lucky the old guy will serenade you with his mandolin. The breakfast is also the best. Not far from there, you should also not miss the tacos from *Taqueria El Rey*.

You often play on Mondays at Motor-City Wine in Corktown. What's so special about Mondays?

MCW has always been very respected and the owners are huge

music fans; Dave is a DJ and obsessed with music. It's very low-key but they used to have nothing on Mondays because it was an industry day. Julian Spradlin, Ryan Spencer and my brother proposed to DJ and make food on this day. It then became one of the most iconic dance nights in the city. I joined later on. It's a mix of house disco, Balearic music, supreme deep cut, YouTube channel shit, and then it ends with dance music. On Wednesday nights, Duality Detroit is incredible. For me this night is Detroit's jam, it should be packed every time. If you don't come on Monday and Wednesday, then, fuck you.

Movement, the techno festival, is one of the main reasons people come to Detroit every summer. What are some afterparties you would never miss?

My first Movement was the first one ever, I was a high school kid, it was free, and we were freaking out! It was the roots. These days I have returned six times to play and it was the beginning of me being an adult in Detroit, not driving my mom's van for days in the city. I know it's cliché but I am very grateful for the festival because it's a catalyst. However, the after-parties are the reason to be over there, so much is going on in so many different pockets.

Is Art Park still one of the Movement after-parties you can't miss out on?

The rising sun party after Movement, starting at 4am is the most iconic party. Just imagine somebody who's not from Detroit walking into an open field, walking on train tracks, waiting for the train to go by, the sky is pink, hundreds of people everywhere. You don't even know where you are, you are next to a huge recycling center, a giant metal structure blowing flames in the sky just inches away from you. It's some Burning Man level shit, but it's so

different because it's so small and in the middle of a city. Everybody is there: the hippie girl, the hip hop crew, the nerds. It goes until 10am and ends with a gospel set. And it's all free. There's also this incredible other spot where Theo Parrish has his afterparty. You can't see the DJs. They're, like, hidden from you. People are there just for the music, you don't know who's playing. It's the purest form of party. It's not about fame or drugs. It's about music, dancing and solidarity. They have two rooms, one is more for deep techno and electro and the other one is an ambient room.

And what about a collective that throws parties all year round?

Freakish Pleasures, which is also organized by Julian Spradlin and Ryan Spencer, is one of the best.

You have your studio, Portage Garage, in Hamtramck, but what's the gallery space like?

My brother and I do exhibitions as well as parties in this old garage that we renovated. There's no schedule. It's a label, a gallery, a home, and a studio.

Do you have any secret parties to tell us about?

I can't give out the secret places. We throw parties all over, but you have to get in contact with us and the locals. It's old school, but still happening.

Mural on the side of Yemen Cafe in Hamtramck

Demographic Splash

Originally home to steel workers from around the globe, these weathered streets were a ghetto for decades. But rapid gentrification has shined light on one of Detroit's most diverse quarters

| Night | Eat, Drink, Dance |

Whether this place is packed to the brim on a Saturday night or just catering to the after-work wino on Monday, you will never find a dull moment at *MotorCity Wine*. Pull up, don't let the semi-drab interior get you down, grab a bottle of Tempranillo, hit the dance floor, lose yourself completely, and be ready to move your feet until they hit the floor of your Checker Cab at the end of the night. Prep your night by listening to *Water* by local electronic-pop band, Jamaican Queens, to start getting to know some of the DJs, producers, and artists that play here weekly. Every monday one DJ brings a pot of his spicy vegan curry that is not to be missed. Every Wednesday the master of the left-hand bass synth, Ian Fink, is there to make you groove out to his magic finger jive.

• MotorCity Wine, 1949 Michigan Ave, Corktown, motorcitywine.com

Back to Green

The city is finally taking advantage of it's empty space, making it greener by the day. In Core City, where once laid a parking lot now is home to a park surrounded by 85 saplings and brutalist concrete benches. A real, normal, safe public park. Detroit needed it and finally has it. Away from the raw atmosphere, get into this little bubble hidden from the streets, where you can sit and enjoy a sandwich from the bakery *Ochre* next door. The owners of Astro Coffee, Jessica Hicks and Dai

Hughes in Corktown decided to expand into this area and open an eatery with real bread. Sourdough is on the menu and the loaf is crispy on the outside and mellow on the inside. Baguettes, focaccia, pita—pick your treat. When beef, pickled carrots, cilantro, mixed greens, and garlic yogurt is added it makes it even more savory. Especially when the produce is sourced from local farms.

• Ochre Bakery and Core City Park, 4884 Grand River Av, Core City, ochrebakery.com

Red Heavan

Home to the Detroit Theater Organ Society, who provides accompaniment to silent movies, the *Senate Theater* gleams and glows through the night with radiant red cultural light. Walking through the great doors of this building feels like being transported into America in the 1930s, especially after passing through the lobby and smelling popcorn and whisky. Sit or stand while you watch, for the old terrace is still present for your perching pleasure. Dress for the occasion, whatever it may be: viewings of short contemporary films by local filmmakers, satellite viewings of international and national film festivals, and films of the past.
• Senate Theater, 6424 Michigan Ave, Southwest, dtos.org

Food **Fresh & Spicy**

Brad Greenhill started in Detroit with a food truck. He has since given it up to became the chef of Takoi, a Thai eatery. The building contrasts it's traditional brick surroundings. Moreover, the interior brings you into a world of tenebrosity and colorful neon light. You'll have the choice between dining in the main room or in the relaxing patio. If you visit the bar be sure to order The Promise in Vortex, a tequila and mezcal infused cocktail with a concoction of Thai chili spices surrounding the rim.
• Takoi, 2520 Michigan Ave, Corktown, takoidetroit.com

Food North of the Border

At *Taqueria* (pictured) you have two different crews: the ones that go there for the corn tortilla tacos and the ones that go there for the barbecue. If you opt for the first be courageous and try the tripe or the tongue to challenge yourself on another culinary plane. If you decide to go with the second option the chicken the most savoury and the ribs most sweet. Or enjoy some basic El Salvadoran treats around the corner: *Pupuseria* is posted up next to an abandoned house and train yard. Make sure to chow down on the pupusas, gluten-free stuffed corn pancakes served with a spicy cabbage salad, and the outstanding fried plantain.
• Taqueria El Rey, 4730 Vernor Hwy; Pupuseria Salvadoreno, 3149 Livernois, Southwest

Night Showtime

The live sets that come through *El Club* are on a par with with those playing at the Filmore and Fox theatre. Take this neon-lined opportunity to see internationally renowned artists like Milo, Princess Nokia, Alex Cameron or Neon Indian in a super intimate setting. And, if your timing is just right you can catch some local legends here too. Push through the crowd, get to the front of the stage, and dance yourself clean.
• El Club, 4114 Vernor Hwy, Southwest, elclubdetroit.com

Diasporic Being

Bryce Detroit
is a storyteller, an Afrofuturist, a Quincy Jones-inspired hip hop artist, an activist, and a pioneer of Entertainment Justice. All in one. Part of the Oakland Avenue Artists Coalition, he is reclaiming the North End through the arts and is giving back to the neighbourhood; redefining the heritage it once possessed. It's already started with The Garage. Throughout his motivation to redesign a cultural infrastructure for Diasporic African narratives, Bryce Detroit is creating a cooperative neighbourhood-based economy

With his desire to honour the legacy of native artists, Jallah Bryce Detroit brings us into the heart and mind of the Afrofuturist. He tells us about the parts of the city that will never be forgotten and how they have evolved

What does The North End represent?

The North End is a neighbourhood in Detroit with a historical community of diasporic Africans and Jews. In the 20th century it was the cultural, creative, and economic hub for black people living in Detroit. It was the people here who opened the first black venues, theatres, and restaurants. The legacy of Motown began here. We had the most important clubs in Detroit, including the one next door—the Apex bar. And I'm proud to say that I am now a part owner of Apex and am developing it back into what it once was. It was well known as a blues bar, starring people like John Lee Hooker. A quarter mile down the road we had Phelps Lounge, which was considered one of the top-tier venues in Detroit. Then there's Berry Gordy of Motown. Berry was methodical in how he promoted his artists. One of his methods was only letting his artists perform in the best venues. BB King, Miles Davis... You didn't have to go to New York.

What is left of Oakland Avenue now?

Well for one thing there's the place you're sitting in right now, *The Garage*. Since 2014 we've hosted a number of awesome parties, and I helped to reactivate this space. But before we could, we needed to figure out how to rebuild the North End's cultural economy. You need to have places where you can experiment and create for free—usually those places were churches or speakeasies. So, for me, phase one was to create a space where people can create and experiment for close to no cost. That's how we came up with The Garage. Since then we have been using this space for experimentation and creation.

What does Afrofuturism mean to you?

It's a label. A label that describes a million-year-old intuitive and indigenous practice. Afrofuturism is acknowledging our moment in time. We are taking the time now to think about how we should interact, associate with, and qualify our environment. Knowing that our behaviour today will have some impact on our future. Afrofuturism is about designing and cultivating identity, on purpose, to have an impact on future generations.

You just participated in the Afrofuturism exhibition at Library Street Collective, what are some of your other favorite galleries?

Norwest Gallery of Art, N'namdi Center for Contemporary Art, and *Playground Detroit*.

Can you tell us about a few artists that people coming to the city should look into?

Three artists that inspire me on a spiritual level and a performance level are: Efe Bes, SuperCoolWicked, and Tunde Olaniran.

You used to live in the University District. Are there any places that you still really love to go to?

In the University District, our main commercial thoroughfare is the Avenue of Fashion. As well as shops along McNichols, which Detroiters culturally refer to as "Six Mile." Along those corridors, some great spots are: *The Narrow Way, Three Thirteen Store*, and *Caribbean Citchen*.

Where would you bring a friend who has never seen Detroit?

On a music point, I'd take them straight to Underground Resistance so that they can learn that techno is a Detroit African music legacy, and the *Motown Museum*. On a cultural tip, I would definitely bring them to the *Dabls Mbad African Bead Museum*

Motown Museum
New Center

Dabls Mbad African
Bead Museum
New Center

so they can experience how dias-poric Africans live in the 21st century when they are investigating and defining what it is to be an African indigenous to Detroit. I would definitely bring them to *Oakland Avenue Urban Farm* and *D-town Farm*. What I really want people to see when they visit is that if you leave us to our own devices we will create economy—regardless of what's around. We've built grassroots economies that are infinitely scal-able. *Artist Village*, on the west side, is a powerful space that's been around for over a decade—it's a real reflection of Detroit ingenuity. Also I strongly recommend folks google historian and scholar Jamon Jordan and schedule one of his amazingly rich and deeply-nuanced Detroit Black History tours.

How would you describe Detroit?

Industrious. Creative in the intu-itive and innate way it pulls you out of your head. And definitely black as fuck. Detroit is a home for inno-vation, social activism, culture, technology, and art—real legacies that Detroit is still known for. I mean, fuck Henry Ford, but he was all about imagination. He came up with the hemp-powered car and then the water-powered one. On a social activism tip, labour movements in the United States as we know them today started here as a result of the great migration caused by the auto industry's promise of the five-dollar work day. The first labour movements began in the basements of our auto plants. You can take that all the way to 2014 when we came together during the Flint water crisis. We were able to raise the narrative to the point where it re-ceived international attention. Where the United Nations finally got wind of it and brought an expert here to speak about the criminal injustices being done by our government.

Where do you see Detroit in the long term? What would be your dream Detroit comeback?

It would have to start with policy. For the last 40 years a lot of people have been identifying with Detroit as a majority black city. But, Detroit has a manufactured majority black population as a result of the real-estate industry in the late 1940s. The advancement of technology cre-ated better opportunities to develop land that would have otherwise remained undeveloped. Those lands are now the suburbs that surround Detroit. So, what people call white flight and how they attribute it to riots, started with real-estate com-panies working with advertising agencies to make up some fliers that basically said—some shit like—"the niggers are coming." In a super segregated and unjust Detroit.

That said, My people started com-ing here in the early 1920s, and there have never been policies on the books to support majority black populations in Detroit. The first time in 100 years that Detroit ever saw policies like that was during the Coleman Young era. And, the moment that he left office, we started experi-encing a systematic destruction of all the policies that he put in place. So in short, my future vision of Detroit starts with all new policies, and an administration that under-stands that the only real way to have a Detroit that changes world culture, is done socially and through policy. And everything else should just fall into place after that.

You are a hip hop musician, what inspires your Music? What do you want to say through your music?

Really quick I want to say that Motown existed at the same time as this other label called Golden World Records—that had Jacky Wilson and Wilson Picket. Berry Gordy stole those guys. So really, Motown was

The Dabls Mbad African Bead Museum built by Olayami Dabls is a sanctuary for raw art

not the only thing happening at the time. But the reason why Motown was so successful is because Detroit had a recording industry ecosystem. I mean shit, that was a black label existing in a violently racist time in Detroit. So like, for Motown to make it, that must mean there was an infrastructure designed not even for black labels.

Personally, I am very interested in making a new pop culture that is grounded in ancestral black energy. And since I am from Detroit, every genre of music out there is in me. One of the ways that we come in contact with all of them is through sampling. My music is reflective of the multiple genres that my people created.

I was recording some of my music out in Dearborn (a Detroit suburb) one day and the engineer looked at me and said "Bryce, your music sounds like techno music," and at the time I was deeply offended. I thought he was telling me that my music sounded corny. But, I hadn't learnt yet that techno started in Detroit and was a black music art. And it took me a long time to realise that it was the kind of music that he was talking about that had been influencing me all those years. But at that time, in 2005, I had only heard the music he was talking about in skating-rinks and in the background of video games. I didn't know that a lot of new-age techno was sampling work that came right out of Detroit.

Where would you go to listen to music?
That is an interesting question in 2019. The reality is, in the late 1990s there were still some good clubs open. There were warehouses and other things that resembled the spirit here. The way that the economic downturn happened—the subprime mortgage fiasco, this predatory capitalism coupled with the auto industry receiving bailouts, yet still firing tens of thousands of people—there was a significant amount of economy and capital lost. So, where you once had people in their 20s and 30s buying and renovating buildings, turning them into venues and sustainable businesses—where you had people with disposable income coming in and patronising those businesses—you now had those same people finding themselves without a disposable income, and those same businesses no longer able to survive. Now, that's really when we started to see a number of those places start to shutter. When there weren't enough people around to support and maintain them, and when folks didn't have money to keep up. But still a great place to listen to hip hop, in a vibrant family-friendly environment is downtown at *Dilla's Delights*. Another one to listen to Detroit music that's masterfully curated is the *Griot Music Lounge*. A good event that takes place every year is the Sidewalk Detroit Festival, the first weekend of August. It's three days packed with music and art performance, visual art and design installations, and an awesome cross-section of Detroiters.

What about some good record shops to go to?
Peoples Records and *Hello Records*.

You talked about creating spaces for musicians and artists. Are there some spaces that give people who don't have the resources access to high-end recording equipment?
Yes, Assemble Sound is a recording studio and licensing agency in Corktown. Their residents and interns are basically able to just hang out all day and put out tracks. I really appreciate the work that Garret (Kohler, Founder of Assemble Sound) is doing there. He is one

A billboard outside Library Street Collective promoting an exhibition on Afrofuturism

of those people who, from some kind of heart-space, is truly inspired to support the new cultural infrastructure here. That kind of space is a really good model of what creative collaborative economies can look like on some bottom-line shit. So in that way his work is, for sure, inspiring. For me though, my interest is first in supporting those who want to create self-determined music economies. Especially as an activist, I like to kindly critique the capitalisation and corporatisation of music. And, that space is one where many people have compromised their music emotionally and spiritually to get there. And then, that music ends up being used to promote consumer behaviours to people who don't have the income to even take part in them.

Doesn't that come back to what you learned about Techno? Video game music and roller-rink music?

It's a double-edged sword. Music goes on TV and in commercials so people can find it and sample it, and in that way it's influential, but my work is a way to navigate these contradictions—staying rooted and centred in our own spiritual and cultural values.

What is the best way to get lost in Detroit?

Relying 100% on Google Maps.

Meeting Coney

Margot Guicheteau

The black and orange leather chairs contrasted against the blue
and pale-yellow mosaic wall, a warm breeze goes from the door on
Lafayette street, all along the corridor of the little restaurant to
the other door on Michigan Avenue. It's still early at Lafayette Coney
Island. Ali and his team are getting ready for the intense lunch
coming up

Just like every other day of the week. The only one that is talking is Romani, an immigrant from Eastern Europe, who comes from time to time to help the team—all Yemenites. He cuts the sausages and can't shut up about Romania. Ali is here to remind him that the United States has welcomed him with open arms. This is Detroit's legacy. Yemeni people working in a restaurant that was once owned by Greek immigrants, who live in Hamtramck, a neighbourhood that used to be inhabited solely by the Polish, and is now occupied by a slew of Middle Eastern communities. A different reality. The one where being American also means coming from somewhere else.

The pile of brownish pink sausages is finally ready. A few clients start to rush in. The routine begins. From one hand to the next, porous bread goes down the assembly line. The sausages in rows, cooked barley brown in a few minutes. As a sleight of hand passes, the sandwich is almost ready. Chili, molten plastic yellow mustard and onion squares cover everything. Done. The dog is dribbling. The plates are sliding down the counter. It's noon in Detroit. It's rush hour. At the counter, greasy fingers are grabbing chili dog after chili dog for $2.60. Only the fingers change. Thick ones, skinny ones, and tiny ones. They are the ones of the blue collar worker, the businessman from Bedrock, and the tourist from Germany. It seems as if they all made an appointment at Coney Island. The rhythm is going crescendo. The waiters are playing the showmen. One is proud of being able to hold seven plates at the same time. Laying them down on his two arms. The other one is showing a customer the fork trick. Where he stacks forks and toothpicks ten high.

The restaurant is getting empty already. They didn't even have time to finish broiling all the sausages, but the customers have already gone back to work. Whatever, it's now going to be calm until the night shift. Ali goes underground for a break, takes off his shoes and looks at a YouTube video of animals fighting. Later on he decides to go back up to chat with his coworkers about a video that he just found: the explanation of the Titanic sinking, in Arabic. The last two customers are debating.

"Lafayette is my Coney Island."
"I still stand for American next door"

A common discussion here. Because coneys are not just coneys.

"So let's go and have one from American"
"Let's do it"

The Lafayette fan swallows the last bite and is ready to, maybe, be converted. Concerned, he follows his friend—really excited.

Just next door, the interior is suddenly all about flash. Checkerboard mosaic for the floor and aluminium boards for the ceiling. The colour red dominates the scene.

"Did you know that this coney is the first one? Keros, a Greek immigrant came to Detroit and opened this restaurant, a few years later he brought his brother who opened the one we were just in."

Coney Island went through all the same storms the city did, yet remains the same. Between 1900 and 1919, 343,000 Greek and Macedonian people arrived, en masse, to the American continent. A lot passed through New York's Ellis Island and got inspired by the already existing Coney Island Dog. They imagined that doing a fast, cheap hot dog for the Motor City workers was going to be a profitable affair. And it was. They spread. Each with their own slightly different recipe.

"I heard that Duly's in South West is also a very iconic one, but for their breakfast."

Out the door again. They were starting a Coney Island competition.

This one is small and only has a counter. A blond woman, with a sweet smile, but a jaded eye, is taking the orders of the very excited duo. "Do you want to add grits?"

They did.

On the walls, three small black and white framed pictures are hanging above them, a big one with nine pictures of Anthony Bourdain, mouth wide open, round big eyes ready to swallow the dog. Next to it, the words he used to describe it: "It seems like a simple thing. Hot dog, chili, raw onions, mustard, steamed bun, but the delicate interplay between these ingredients when done right is symphonic." I thought it was just a hot dog. Not a classical orchestra.

A young boy is staring at it while eating one, almost mimicking the same face in the picture. The duo makes the connection and have a good laugh about it. They start interacting and all seem to get along pretty well. Twenty minutes later the boy jumps in his truck followed by the two coney island fans. After a short drive, they enter a big warehouse, on which is written Ross Coated Fabrics. In the back, a pile of yellow foam. A tall, robust man is cutting a coach with a dirty-green rusted machine.

"Tim, this guy from Hamtramck brought this oriental coach to cut up, I'll let you finish. Who are those two guys you are with?"

Very candidly, he answers, "Just two New Yorkers who came to eat the best coney around. And they still can't shut up about it."

That's what happens when you go from hot dog to hot dog. You end up in a fabric warehouse.

Margot Guicheteau is a French journalist who has written for French national newspaper "Le Figaro" and "Le Temps" in Switzerland. She moved three years ago to Detroit, exploring her Polish roots among the US's second largest community while documenting the city's unique and complex history.

Roslyn Karamoko
When she imagined "Détroit Is The New Black" it was just a casual t-shirt company. It is now a platform for fashion designers around the world to test their products in a new emerging market, based out of a high-end boutique on Woodward Avenue in Downtown Detroit

Roslyn Karamoko, Owner, Détroit is the New Black

Fashion Geek

Even if Detroit is not famous for shopping, Roslyn Karamoko knows where to look to find what's fashionable. She reveals the real vintage shops for those who want to prance around brimming with flair and elegance from Detroit's golden age

You're from Seattle, what brought you here?

I arrived here in 2013, and there was really not much going on in the way of fashion. Shinola was just starting around that time, but I thought there was a real opportunity for something more. Historically Detroit is very blue collar, but I knew there was a new demographic on its way in, so I thought of doing something a little more cosmopolitan. So, I started to make t-shirts and it just kind of worked. At first I just gave them out to friends as Christmas gifts, but then people started to ask where they could buy more. That's when I took them online. Then in some little pop-ups in Eastern Market. Then I opened a little shop in Namadi Gallery in Midtown. Around this time Bedrock started to develop downtown and I thought of asking them for this warehouse space. It was so huge that I created this kind of exhibition-style, community retail model and started to bring in more designers and small businesses. Now we are more like an accelerator for small retail businesses. We house local and national designers who want to test the Detroit market. It's exciting for them to be able to use our platform, and the attraction of the brand, to allow their businesses to get in front of new customers. We sell casual basic t-shirts for $29, denim, candles, as well as some accessible luxury. We are creating a space that feels upscale, and is, but also isn't. The name is not about fashion, it's about connectivity. It's a vehicle to bring people here from everywhere.

Who are the latest designers you've discovered and brought to the store?

I'm really excited about Brother Valleys from New York. She sources her accessories and materials from artisans all over Africa. It's expensive but it's more like art. Tracy Reese, from Detroit, is one of the designers who had the opportunity to dress Michelle Obama, and did a sustainable capsule for us that she produced in Michigan.

Do you also host events?

Yes, we do music events on the first Friday of every month, and we do wellness events every third Thursday. We also just opened a little local coffee shop in our boutique called Coffee Haus.

What do you think Detroit needs?

We need some black people ownership downtown for one thing. That an obvious statement though. It's also the point of this brand, I don't shy away from the racial conversation that our name brings to the table. You hear "the new black" all the time, but when you put Detroit in front of it, it changes everything. It can have so many different connotations. But in this city it really makes sense. It's very intentional and it gets people to stop and think for a second. It's how I'm trying to include a minority in a meaningful way. Long story short, having a larger percentage of minority-run businesses downtown is very important. Especially when this huge Hudson project is about to be built.

The problem is that black people here don't own their own businesses. When I was growing up in Seattle, it was very hippie, crunchy, and there was a kind of similar sense of community that we have in Detroit. It has this big city, small town feeling. What is happening here, in terms of gentrification, has happened in so many other cities. I am trying to forecast that. What a changing city needs to really retain the original talents is culture—it's always a testing ground. There are so many incubators here but no real

The Heidelberg Project: an entire neighbourhood transformed into an art installation for the preservation of the community market. It's very scary to see that the economy is almost entirely reliant on one person—Dan Gilbert. And, we ask ourselves the question: where do we all fit in here? I am not sure about the future, but I know that there's a community energy here and now. People support authenticity and it's why we are so successful.

What other minority-run businesses located downtown can you recommend?
   House of Pure Vin, The Lip Bar, the TEN.

What are some of the things you admire about Detroit?
   It's inspiring to see so many homegrown brands, companies, and innovative minds in one place. Detroit has people that just make shit happen. It's still the idea of the American Dream. Where can that still happen? It already happened almost everywhere else in the country. Here you can literally sell t-shirts out of the trunk of your car and then be here on Woodward Avenue next to Le Labo one year later.

What would be your advice to a foreigner arriving here?
   Don't stay downtown. Rent a car, check out Livernois Avenue which was pretty much the avenue of fashion, and is now trying to be redeveloped. You'll find old school suit companies, blue hats, ties. I really like to eat at *Kuzzo's Chicken and Waffles* as well as *Good Cakes and Bakes.*

Is there a real fashion identity in the city?
   Detroit is super fancy and super fly. There's a real flair in Detroit. It's old school cosmopolitan. You dress up, you shine your shoes, and in winter you wear your fur just to go grocery shopping.

If you were to name two spots to check out for a fancy night in Detroit, what would they be?
   Cliff Bell's, a jazz bar as well as *Parc,* a beautiful restaurant for dinner located in Campus Martius.

What are some great places to shop around the city?
   Mama Coo's Boutique is the best, I also love *The Velvet Tower.*

If there was one present a tourist should buy in Detroit what would it be?
   The *Détroit is the New Black* t-shirt!

What are the two most iconic places in the city?
   Belle Isle is beautiful, it's a natural preserved spot. *The Heidelberg Project,* is just a raw and honest body of work.

Is there a little known authentic place you love to go to?
   The restaurant *Sinbad's,* an old school family run spot. You have to try the frog legs.

What does Detroit mean to you?
   Detroit is beautiful and complex. It's a real mind trick. Detroit has a lot of baggage.

The project was initiated in 1986 by Tyree Guyton who painted bright dots on houses on Heidelberg Street

Pastel Mortar

A showcase by Eleanor Oakes

Born in New York, Oakes spent some time in California paying attention to the colourful, graffiti-stained and paint-patched walls. After moving to Detroit she noticed the walls here had a different kind of patchwork. Each new layer showed the evolution of the building and, by extension, the city's recovery. This led to her collection "Removed."

Philip Kafka is an investor who made his fortune in the New York City ad game. He found an opportunity to start a new chapter in Detroit. First he built Takoi, a darling of the city's trendy set. Then, alongside architect Edwin Chan, he imagined and built a little village of Quonset hut homes. His optimism knows no bounds, and is now giving Core City the jolt it's been waiting for. Most of his projects are developed with his dear friend Ish Rafiuddin, an architect who began his career in New York and now has his own studio called Undecorated

Ish Rafiuddin & Philip Kafka

Urban Transcendence

Detroit is their playground, a city where all remaining vacancies are reimagined as greenspace and parkland—giving abandoned buildings a new pulse. They dream of trees in the in-betweens, challenging the dystopic vision of Detroit. Together they break the rules to build a micro-city for the future

How did you two meet?

Ish: We met in Turkey. Philip's best friend and I met as expats in Istanbul and we became really good friends. I was working on a project in Turkey for a New York office. I met Philip when he came to visit his best friend, who was also in Istanbul.

Philip: I had a business in New York, a media agency. I would go around the city with a zoning map and call the owners of buildings that had the right zoning for an advertising sign. I would call and say "I want to rent your wall." My whole idea was to rent the exterior walls of these buildings for twenty years and then rent them to companies as advertising space.

How did the story continue?

Ish: When I came back from Istanbul, Philip and I reconnected in New York and became friends, too.

Philip: And I needed architectural drawings for the sign permits, so we started talking. This job was not for him. However, it was the beginning of us knowing each other. I got to understand real estate through walls, and when my business became successful, I went around the country to find more.

Is that how you discovered Detroit?

Philip: Yes. I went to a lot of cities, and Detroit was the most interesting. Many parts of the city looked war torn in 2012, many parts still do. I just started driving around. I didn't really understand it. No one around. Should I feel safe here? I didn't know. I visited twelve times, a weekend per month. Slowly, I felt more comfortable, and then the first building I bought is where my restaurant Takoi is, near Corktown, and then Ish heard I was going to build a restaurant and he told me that he wanted to do the design for it. And he did.

Ish: I knew very little about Detroit, I came once when I was a child in the 1990s; I remember it was very empty. It was known to have houses that you could buy for very cheap, just with cash. When I came back for Takoi I realised there was just a lot to do in terms of design.

What is the idea behind Takoi?

Ish: The idea is to create a renewed sense of excitement for Detroit. It also needed to be flexible, malleable, with a lean construction budget. Also, there is a dialogue between old and new; if something was already existing and was working, we kept it and celebrated it as part of the design. The intervention was utilitarian but also flexible for future possibilities. Philip gave me two rules that were not to be broken: one, there was to be an open kitchen, and two, no chairs... only booths. For me architecture is thinking about all the little details, so I liked this challenge.

Philip: Originally Takoi was going to be a diner so we kept the idea of having booths, but Ish was able to bring it to a different level when we decided to make it a Thai restaurant. People complain every now and again because the booths are tight, but I'll be honest, I don't really care when people complain about stuff we put so much thought and effort into. The only thing is that we must be excellent with the essentials, in order to be quirky in certain regards. No, you must be the best at what you do, when you are breaking rules. The third rule I gave him was that nobody can look at walls. Everyone is meant to have a view. It is the same thing at Magnet, our new restaurant. All booths, open kitchen, and no one looking at a wall. Who wants to look at a wall when they're out?

Diego Rivera's fresco "Detroit Industry Murals" at the Detroit Institute of Arts (DIA)

Urban Transcendence

What inspires you in Detroit?

Ish: I am inspired by the "dystopic" Detroit, it's fascinating because it says that it's okay to not fit in, and it's okay to be different. There's no right way to do things. We can use cheap materials to make interesting structures, we can celebrate an old wall because it has character, and we can lead people to be more interactive with space. That is kind of "dystopic" because they are in a territory beyond their comfort zone.

Philip: When you play by standard rules, you get judged by standard fields. This field is broken; this is an atypical place. In Detroit there's a culture of experimentation from Henry Ford with the automobile to Motown to house music. Even the Nation of Islam started here with their ideas and ideology. Detroit has always been a home to ideas. With a million dollars, it is more interesting to buy something for almost nothing in Detroit, and invest your dollars in what you build, not what you buy. In New York you spend all of your money just getting the property, and have little left to really engage in creative practices. I love the challenge. It's fun. Also, we are the minority here, it's an 82% black city, it's another challenge to communicate your ideas to a demographic that comes from a totally different place than you. Imagine how a young black person feels in a white America. It's interesting to learn the landscape as a minority, respect it, and then learn to work with it.

What is the secret to being successful here?

Philip: The secret is to do what you believe in. When I meet with the community, they have never considered anything like what I am showing them. I frequently doubt our ideas, which leads me to be sensitive to the doubts of others.

Through hearing the community, I learn how to make our projects better than they already are and to communicate their intent. It's hard to make everyone as excited about an idea as I can be, but we take it on and I love it. I go to community meetings and I get beat up. But I am like a fighter. I go to those meetings knowing the sport and where the punches are coming from. I know I am going to get hit, so I have to do my sit ups before I go into the ring. I am prepared. The city inspires a lot of ideas, but it also inspires you to let them go... it's a tough place. You better be prepared for a boxing match! People see the opportunity, but it doesn't mean it's easy. A lot of people that come here are very optimistic, but optimism isn't enough, you need grit to make it in Detroit.

What is your intention in developing the whole neighbourhood of Core City?

Philip: I want to build projects that people have never built. I want to create common spaces that are extremely special. I like Core City because it had a lot of space, and little to no commercial activity when I arrived. I liked this intersection, the train tracks, and there were still enough buildings to make something happen.

Ish: The primary streets have Albert Khan's buildings; the secondary streets have factories; the tertiary streets have houses. I am really interested in the tertiary streets. This is where 99% of the people are. These are the streets that have wide open greenery and trees. There are about 100,000 vacant lots in Detroit, and when you're in the middle of it you feel like you are in the prairie. Whatever you do, you have to incorporate the land. That's what Core City Park is all about. The park was originally an underused asphalt parking lot, so we

The Continental, an abandonned factory that might become a night club soon

worked with that and turned it into a public green space. I also like the pockets and the in between spaces. I don't believe in the idea that the whole city will be filled up by new buildings and people. There's already so much that is not. Detroit is like 75% vacant, so we have to think about it and use it in our design and build as many parks as possible.

Philip: Landscape is a way of being generous. Trees are everything. Architecture gets you excited about the present moment. Trees make you excited about the future.

You just bought an enormous abandoned engine factory called the Continental just outside Jefferson Chalmers. What are you going to do with it?

Philip: To think that this was available for me to buy is just crazy. I feel like I bought the Colosseum. I can't believe it. If we develop

Continental the right way, people from all over the world will want to come. The building is a monument. What should an industrious kid, like me, do with a monument. Nothing typical—forget festivals, and all those traps. Let's think beyond the zeitgeist. This building inspires and demands that.

Do you feel that Detroit is the next Berlin?

Philip: Detroit and Berlin were both built on faulty ambition, built for many more people than they currently house. Both cities over-expanded during the early to mid 20th century with questionable ambitions and methods. I think that when you want too much, too quickly, you fail. You can feel the ghosts of the past in both cities. Electronic music at night sounds good in both cities, too.

Ish: There's a similarity in the spatial qualities and the emptiness. They're both low density, with low-rise buildings, spaced out and covering a lot of territory, with small lakes all around, and a similar climate.

What do you think about what Dan Gilbert, the biggest investor in Detroit, is doing downtown?

Philip: His work is good and valuable, but it's not original. I don't think it captures the true opportunity that exists in a place like Detroit. He's building the tallest building in Michigan where the famous Hudson's Department Store once was. Imagine this: he should use the sunken site, as is, and build a park in it. If he did that, then suddenly very sophisticated people from all over the world would come to Detroit. They would think: "If they took the most valuable piece of land in the city and turned it into a park it must be something special, I've got to go see this park!" And in Detroit, Dan Gilbert would be able to do this because he owns everything else around it, and this move would elevate those property values. Honestly, who is going to be interested in the biggest skyscraper in Michigan? Very few interesting people, it's the same game developers have been playing in more standard markets for decades. On the other hand, I am sure I'll use what he's bringing into downtown—maybe an Equinox, or an Apple Store. But, we need a balance between what is useful and what has character, what is everywhere, and what can only be in Detroit. Detroit presents an interesting opportunity because it is so unique. Think about it like this: if you try to normalise the bizarre in you, you become a soft version of something weird; but, if you really lean into being bizarre, you can become special, something that no one has ever seen. In Detroit, people are trying to normalise this bizarre place, and if you try to do that you are going to end up with just another place. I don't want Detroit to feel like Chicago and New York. We have to find and keep the bizarreness of this city.

Ish: I think whatever people are doing in Detroit, it's already a big step. I don't feel they are linked to heritage, so they are more open to modernity. It's good what Dan Gilbert is doing. Like this, we can do all the interesting stuff. It all makes sense in the end.

What words would you use to describe Detroit?

Philip: Space, wilderness, exoticism, dystopia, utopia. I travel a lot. I am always happy when I come back here. It's not about money; it's about vision. Before the rule in real estate was: location, location, location. For me, this rule doesn't exist anymore. Now, it's quality, quality, quality. Because of Google Maps, you see the reviews and how the business is judged. You'll go to the best one wherever it is. People who are here are pioneers and there aren't that many, so you feel a sense of connectivity. Here everybody is connected, because we all made the choice to come to this challenging city, a city that is so different from all the others. We are more interested in what we can make and experience than what we can consume.

If you had a whole full day without having to work, what would you enjoy doing?

Philip: Start by running in Lafayette Park where you'll see Mies Van der Rohe's buildings, then on the Dequindre Cut, down to the river toward Belle Isle, the whole loop of Grand Boulevard. You'll also see

A Quonset hut home in Core City's True North

the beauty of the island, of the old mansions, then you'll go to the rough parts, and then the abandoned Packard Plant, which is way more industrial. You'll finish in Hamtramck. Running in Detroit is special—you don't have people to give you energy in this city, so you have to find it, and once you do, you feel tough. You'll feel invigorated. When I am done, I love to go to Trinosophes and have a coffee, talk to people, and engage with them.

And what about a place to have a snack?

Philip: You have to go to the Telway on Michigan Avenue for the hamburgers; it's cute! I also love the Zen Center in Hamtramck, lunch only.

What about you, Ish?

Ish: I would walk to Clique diner for an amazing breakfast. It's one of the most authentic places in Detroit. You experience the energy of the people who live here. It's a good representation of the Detroit demographic. Then, walk up to Eastern Market and shop during the weekend. In the afternoon, I often love to go to the DIA (Detroit Institute of Arts) for their world renowned art collection.

Philip: They have the greatest hits, all the modernists! Isn't Ish the greatest guy?!

Downtown

Kept Alive

Downtown Detroit is more alive than it has been in decades. The epic monuments of empire that survived here are finally being renovated, allowing new businesses to thrive in a place that wildlife had started to reclaim just a few years ago

| Culture | What's Happening

Library Street Collective is Detroit's true gallery of contemporary art, and owners JJ and Anthony Curis have done an amazing job at curating the best of the best in contemporary art from locally and nationally known artists. Their interior space transforms for every show to properly accommodate whatever work they might be exhibiting. Since their business is an extension of The Belt, a built-out back alley full of bars and restaurants in downtown, they are able to host worthwhile openings, events, and parties that utilise space in some of the most ritualistic and high-tech ways possible. As a collective, LSC is able to work with local businesses to make sure that their walls are also covered with what's right in the art world. Collaborating with artists, business owners, and designers, they are on the cutting edge, restoring Detroit to its rightful place in the panorama of US contemporary art.
• Library Street Collective,1260 Library St, Downtown, lscgallery.com

Cards on the Table

With prohibition long gone, some locals felt that part of the city's charm had died along with it. So they found a closet behind an old skyscraper and proposed something special: a modern speak-easy. Every drink in this joint is themed with a tarot card and comes with a little something special. When you sit down, you're brought a seasonal apértif on the house. You can get anything from the most basic dry gin martini to a cashew-smoked Manhattan coined The Hammer. And for those with elite gangster credentials, look up to the top shelf for vintage spirits—at $200 per 20oz.
• Bad Luck Bar, 1218 Griswold St, Downtown, bad-luckbar.com

Night **From Ghosts to Goths**

Up the sprawling stairs, a woman dressed in black, wearing tattoos instead of sleeves, welcomes you to a decrepit luxurious hall, while asking for your ID. Once a lavish hotel, nightclub and hiding place for the Purple Gang and Jimmy Hoffa, gossipers always loved to talk about how haunted this place is. This didn't scare German developer Mike Higgins, however, who opened the club here in 1983. Since then it has evolved, always keeping the raw Detroit spirit, and honouring industrial techno, as well as hosting goth parties. Enjoy this huge basement where the high ceilings remind you that it was once a ballroom for the supreme elite.
• Leland City Club, 400 Bagley St, Downtown

Night · Culture **Third Eye**

Detroit's *Masonic Temple* is the biggest of its kind in the world. Just sign up for the architecture tour, which takes place once a month, to take in the enormity of this historic structure in person. Be patient, you'll need around four hours to see less than half of it. If you're lucky, they'll show you the old and completely empty swimming pool. Another option is to come for concerts or the super iconic Movement (DEMF) afterparty, but don't lose track of the agenda!
• Masonic Temple, 500 Temple St, Brush Park themasonic.com

A long line outside *Clique* is normal, and regulars don't mind the wait. You and plenty others in the city want to be part of this clique. The place is small, packed, and has no air conditioning. But, you'll have real diner food that's surprisingly grease-free, and served on vintage Fiesta dinnerware. Most of the time your meal comes with pancakes. If it doesn't, be sure to ask for them with an additional topping of bananas or blueberries.

• Clique, 1326 E Jefferson Ave, Island View

Food | Rum Pirates

In 2010 restaurateurs Joe Giocamino and John Vermiglio came from Chicago to Detroit to meet some friends and were brought to the only high-end restaurant outside of Downtown. The food was good but the wait was so long that they made a bet to do better. And they did. *Grey Ghost* is now the place for local yuppies who have an appreciation for perfectly cooked and seasoned meat and seafood. If you are up for it and willing to spend a few extra dollars, make sure to stop by this gentry gem and grab yourself an old fashioned and a filet mignon.

• Grey Ghost, 47 Watson St, Brush Park, greyghostdetroit.com

Shop | Glazed Empire

Pewabic Pottery is a longstanding Detroit institution for the design and production of ceramics of all kinds. Their brick and mortar location is just off Jefferson in West Village and has a first floor shop, second floor gallery, and third floor school for those of you who are spending more than a few days in the city. Newly renovated and stacked high with old school and new age kilns, take a tour of their fabrication room and glazing studio.

• Pewabic Pottery, 10125 E Jefferson Ave, Indian Village, pewabic.org

Treasure Hunting

You would think that one of the top 5 largest bookstores in the world would be at least a little organized, right? Wrong. *John King Books* is composed of two-story warehouses right off the highway. The first building is always publicly accessible and comes equipped with a permanent leak over the Christian Religious Texts, and crotchety half-conscious little helpers dressed up in bright orange aprons, manned with state of the art walkie talkies. The second building houses Mr. King's rare book collection and all the other precious antiques he's collected since 1971, when he opened his first shop in the suburbs of Detroit. When you arrive you'll be handed a map to help you find your way around this labyrinth. Now, better be ready to stay for at least five hours—entrenched in mystic books and some real treasures. A true one was an original photo of Mark Twain found tucked behind the cover of one of his biography's. Another was a small pamphlet from the 1950's signed by John F. Kennedy. You just never know what's hidden in between the lines.

• John K. King Used & Rare Books,
901 W Lafayette Blvd

Paulina Petoski & Samantha Bankle Schefman,
Owners, Playground Detroit

Home is Where the Art is

Paulina Petoski, the daughter of Macedonian immigrants, and Samantha Bankle Schefman, an NY native who spent most of her life in Detroit, see only the best in their city. After studying fashion and jewellery respectively, they returned to their hometown to embark on a joint journey of exhibiting Detroit's potential through its one-of-a-kind creators. Together, they founded Playground Detroit, a platform designed for the promotion of Detroit artists

Always in contact with creatives of all kinds, galleries, and DIY spaces, these two women know what deserves proper attention. With their sometimes conflicting views, they take us on a jaunt through Detroit's contemporary art scene

MOCAD
Midtown

David Klein Gallery
Downtown

**Simone DeSousa
Gallery**
Midtown

Cranbrook
Bloomfield Hills

What Pipeline
Southwest

CAVE
North End

KO Studio
Hamtramck

Grey Area
Southwest

**Eldorado General
Store**
Corktown

How would you describe Playground Detroit?

Paulina: We are a creative platform and an agency for emerging talents in the city of Detroit.

Samantha: And our goal is to attract and retain talent in Detroit.

How does Detroit inspire you?

Paulina: For me growing up and going to DIY art spaces throughout high school and college showed me how to make this city into something different. It was carte blanche, there was nothing to do, nowhere to go. You had to make your own events and your own venues, so the creativity that came out of that was really incredible. Artists were creating environments that were authentic. Whereas in Brooklyn and Manhattan it felt like people were just feeding into the hype, and it was super oversaturated. The reason I wanted to start Playground in New York was to bring Detroit's "je ne sais quoi" to New York. Detroit has this holistic approach of arts and culture that needs to be shared.

What does Detroit need?

Paulina: We need more people, a bigger market, more collectors.

Samantha: We need national attention. Tourism is critical.

What does Detroit have that you can't find anywhere else in the world?

Paulina: Stoplights that dance to electronic music, empty highways and people that won't stop moving and shaking, no matter what.

Samantha: Our rich cultural history: Motown, techno, architecture, art, and a battle to rise from the ashes has created a woven community that champions its colleagues.

What is the best way of getting lost in Detroit?

Samantha: The art galleries have spread themselves throughout every pocket of the city, and you might literally get lost finding them. You'll end up exploring each unique neighbourhood and find there are lovely little shops, delectable cafés and restaurants, and impressive architecture in each. Detroit sits on a large footprint, a car is definitely useful in seeing it all.

What are some of the best places in Detroit to discover art and culture?

Samantha: *The Museum of Contemporary Art Detroit* (MOCAD), *David Klein, Simone de Sousa. Cranbrook* in the suburbs is one of the most prestigious graduate programmes for fine art in the country. Their campus is open to the public and has amazing gardens, creeks, museums, galleries, and their own collector's vault. Everyone from the Detroit art scene goes to Cranbrook shows. But *What Pipeline* in Southwest is really special. They just have one room, but it's always curated beautifully. Every Friday the *Detroit Institute of Arts* is open late you can relax in the courtyard and walk around all the hidden corners. They usually have incredible public programming in the Diego Rivera court.

Paulina: As far as galleries run by artists you have *CAVE* at the Russell Industrial Center and *KO Studio* gallery in Hamtramck.

Paulina, you started in the fashion industry, where would you recommend shopping in the city?

Paulina: We would love to have more boutiques here, but I really love *Grey Area* and *Eldorado General Store*.

And what about your favourite places in general?

Paulina: I love *Kiesling* bar.

Samantha: I always love to shop at *Nora*.

Chene and Farnsworth may be quiet and desolate, but Raven Lounge is still popping

And some more hidden spots?

Paulina: *Donovan's Pub, Bumbo's. Cliff Bell's* is another real Detroit place to listen to jazz.

Samantha: Oh no I don't like the food. I prefer to go to *Raven Lounge*, have shitty fries and dance with people. We have very different tastes.

What keeps you going?

Samantha: I finally became overwhelmed by New York. I see Detroit unfolding the way we dreamed it would. It's going to be tough, but that's what keeps me going. That is why I got into the real estate business. I will always have one ear at the door, trying to understand what is happening, and responding to it. I feel a kind of new wave every time I see the city blooming.

Paulina: There's not a lot of cities that are experiencing such fast change. I love it here because it's exciting. As of last year we put over a quarter million dollars in the pockets of artists directly. I'm pushing to double that by next year.

Do you have a special memory in Detroit that really shows the evolution of the city?

Paulina: I remember looking down from my dad's building into Campus Martius. Campus Martius was not what it is now. There was not a soul. There was a Tall and Easy Shoe Company. I would look around and wonder what was going to become of this place. Now that shoe company is a LuluLemon. Two blocks down there's an H&M about to open. If you told me that when I was sitting on that stoop, I would have laughed in your face. These aren't the things that excite me about Detroit.

Andrew D. Olivo mourns the death of an old self at What Pipeline

Home is Where the Art is

Sound On

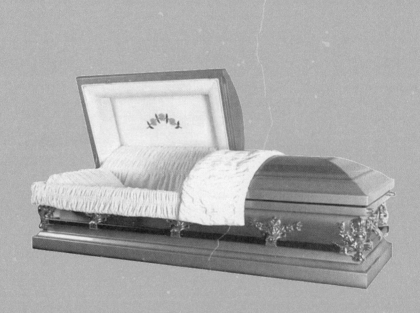

Salem
• Tiny Jag, 2019
Full of spunk, Jillian Graham took her influence from the king of kitch's number one hit Mr. Boombastic, and brought rap to a new level. Tint Jag is super raw, super trappy, and super curt. Polly knew her granddaughter would be something truly unique, and she is.

Books

The Dream Is Now
• Michel Arnaud, 2017

It's no secret that Detroit is a new playground for urban renewal. This book highlights some of the most beautiful and just plain cool ways that people have been going about renovating and reappropriating space.

The Ruins Of Detroit
• Thomas Sugrue, Robert Polidori, Yves Marchand and Romain Meffre 2010

Detroit locals despise the new wave of ruin porn that has dominated the tourism of their city. Well, this book highlights all the objectified destroyed palaces scattered around Detroit's vacant landscape.

Detroit, I do mind dying
• Dan Georgakas, 1975

Through interviews and commentary, the remarkable story of Detroit's Dodge Union Movement and the League of Revolutionary Black Workers unfolds to reveal their significance in the political landscape of the 1960s and 1970s.

Dancing in the Street: Motown and the Cultural Politics of Detroit
• Suzanne E. Smith, 1999

Travel back to Detroit in the 1960s, to follow the story of Motown's evolution from a small record company to an international music industry behemoth, firmly rooted in the African American community.

Films

Only Lovers Left Alive
• Jim Jarmusch, 2014
Vampires suck. But Jim Jarmusch knew just how to play with them. The tale of these two lovers straddles Detroit and Tangier, exploring the musical and emotional ties of everything involved.

Detropia
• Heidi Ewing & Rachel Grady, 2012

As every other major city in America has reached its final destination on the road of gentrification, Detroit stands out as a place where gentry-folk and sustainable economies just don't quite fit in. This documentary tells the tale of this paradox.

Searching For Sugar Man
• Malik Bendjelloul, 2012

In 1970s Detroit Sixto Rodriguez signed two of his albums with Motown. Unfortunately, for him and his career, this did not help it take off. Rumours said that he killed himself. Nevertheless, in South Africa, without knowing it, he became a national icon against apartheid. A few years later, two fans decided to search for him. That's where this story begins.

Music

First Floor
• Theo Parrish, 1998

Parrish is all about representing all things "real" through sound. First Floor is one of his electric-deep house albums from 1998. Released just four years after his move to Detroit, you can hear the influence of the city.

Whatcha See is Whatcha Get
• The Dramatics, 1971

The name of a group and an album have never paired so well. The Dramatics are the kings, princes, dukes, and jesters of Motown drama.

Summer like the Season
• Thin Today, 2017

Most adequately described as experimental art rock, Summer Krinsky plays with live instrumentation, ethereal vocals, and modern electronics.

8641 Linwood Street

Isaac Pickell

8641 Linwood Street

offers a panorama of unthreatening silence
filled by unkempt grass growing so verdant it
distracts from the mournfulness you expect to
internalize here. at the brightest corner there
was a lobby in the dead hotel that smells like moss
and looks like you might expect. two women
work its desk, the taller one bends deeply to
sweep where the rug stops, using a handheld
broom and dustpan set made for a smaller space;
she lets out a groan of necessary complaint with
each stroke. fourteen of the men and women who
live here are regulars of the lobby and six chil-
dren of different men or women come each
Thursday for warm chocolate cookies and cold
whole milk. the dead hotel has three different
carafes used solely for milk, rotated faithfully
each Thursday until dusk because the woman who
does not sweep, the woman who first imagined
warm cookies and cold milk for the far end of the
reception desk, a space that always felt underused
to her, a waste of unscuffed laminate, prefers
the way cold milk looks like it tastes when there's
ample and fresh condensation budding from
the carafe, big beads inflating all along the glass
but not yet pooling around the bottom, and so
the dead woman rotates the carafes each hour
before this puddle forms, a power struggle
between the ceiling fan and the weather forecast
and the electric bill her boss' boss opens. the
milk is very cold. sometimes, the men and women
take the milk in simple, stout paper cups and
drink slowly while sitting in overstuffed green
chairs that don't yet look

like moss
a life without
regret is a life

spent without
desire   the city fills
it self with churches

you may build if
you weren't allowed
a history   there is no room for

small talk when cracking
open an amethyst, or you
will almost never find a butterfly across the
street beside tired houses where Marty welcomes
us to a neighborhood we already live in with her
loving husband and stay-at-home son, across from
a repurposed church of unknown purpose still

draped in Christmastime relics and yesterday's
rainfall. Her words are muffled, covered in
breezes as the grass flutters, with no mind to the
direction of the wind. We slow her floating, full
of childhood dreams, with hope: don't you just love
it here. She chews dismembered holiday spirits,
thinks us over, invites us to follow

spring cleanings clinging to a compost pile
that hides behind a broken tree swing. Missing
a seat, links, and more. A broken extension cord
is hanging from the bough. It must have proved
an unworthy fix and is heavy with unplugged,
untangled, Christmas lights. Families lived here
once upon a time, she says. A lunch box rests
between two beer bottles, childhood shrunken
into a few mottled square feet. There is a warped
foosball table without its legs, abandoned
bleached wood, illuminated garbage. The side door
is left open behind a screen. The overhang leaks.
Hula hooping Mother Mary watches our prog-
ress, her pinwheels shining between cloud cover
against the back wall of the old sea foam church.
We follow

a slow saunter over dirty caterpillar bug
boxes leading us to three addresses on one door:
transient numbers tacked on by transient occu-
pants who shared a communal plastic savings
account in the lifeless back ard. She thinks things
out there need to change. Our generation.
Loosely defined, she gestures at a house across
the way whose towering magnolia has finally
caught up to the height of its decaying landlord.
Histories of taste are visible here through the
duplex's peeling paint. She is dressed in 1-2-3-4-5
she counts five shades of green, her legs are
tanned, she puffs on unlit ashes. Her wedding
happened during Thanksgiving Dinner where
they traded books and exchanged I-do's because
she doesn't like cake. They still write notes about
their love. She thinks we could do better. Do
everything outside the box and you will be just
fine, she says

do you follow? The struggle is finding the
edges, and the bravery to jump them. We leave
with one of the dirty caterpillar bug boxes.

*Born in Ann Arbor, Michigan and raised out back of
his father's second-hand bookstore, Isaac Pickell
is a biracial poet and PhD student of literary and
cultural studies at Detroit's Wayne State University.
His work focuses on the borderlands of blackness
and black literature.*

Available from LOST iN

...and Austin, Dusseldorf, Edinburgh, Helsinki, Marseille, Oslo, Porto, Reykjavik, Rom, Rotterdam, Seattle, Tangier, Tel Aviv in the LOST iN Mobile App

LOSTIN.COM